THIS → OR THAT? History Edition

Enduring the
OREGON TRAIL

A This or That Debate

by Jessica Rusick

T0025630

CAPSTONE PRESS
a capstone imprint

Capstone Captivate is published by Capstone Press, an imprint of Capstone.
1710 Roe Crest Drive
North Mankato, Minnesota 56003
www.capstonepub.com

Library of Congress Cataloging-in-Publication Data is available on the Library of Congress website.
ISBN: 978-1-4966-8390-8 (library binding)
ISBN: 978-1-4966-8788-3 (paperback)
ISBN: 978-1-4966-8441-7 (eBook PDF)

Summary: Thousands of Americans migrated west on the Oregon Trail in the 1800s. Test your decision-making skills with this or that questions related to their journey!

Image Credits
Flickr: Baker County Tourism, 4–5, 14; iStockphoto: Keith Lance, 25; Library of Congress, 9; National Park Service: National Register of Historic Places Digital Archive, 16; Shutterstock: andreiuc88, 29, Bilal Kocabas, 28, Cattallina, 11 (hat), Charles Knowles, 27, D.Semra, 10, DMartin09, 8, Everett Collection, 6, 7, Gchapel, 19, I. Pilon, Cover (background), 32, Imfoto, 15, itzuki87, 24, Jim Lambert, 13, JPL Designs, 3, Krasnova Ekaterina, Cover (monument), Lee Prince, 22, Maria Dryfhout, 26, Neil Webster, Cover (covered wagon), poupine, 18, Robert Adrian Hillman, 11, Russ Heinl, 17, SergeyKlopotov, Cover (barrel), Simon Maddock, 23, StudioKampOC, 20, trinessimo, Cover (bull), 30, Vladimir Konstantinov, 12, Wayne Broussard, 21, Zoran Milic, 5 (map)

Design elements: I. Pilon/Shutterstock (background map)

Editorial Credits
Editor: Rebecca Felix; Designers: Aruna Rangarajan & Tamara JM Peterson; Production Specialist: Tori Abraham

All internet sites appearing in back matter were available and accurate when this book was sent to press.

A DANGEROUS JOURNEY WEST

From the 1840s to 1860s, hundreds of thousands of **pioneers** traveled west on the Oregon Trail. They hoped to make better lives in Oregon or California. They sold their homes and many belongings to buy supplies for the five-to-six-month trip. These supplies included a wagon, oxen, and food.

The Oregon Trail was more than 2,000 miles (3,200 kilometers) long. It crossed mountains, rivers, and deserts. Travelers faced illnesses, accidents, and bad weather. Most started new lives in the west. But more than 20,000 people died during the journey.

HOW TO USE THIS BOOK

What if you had been a traveler on the Oregon Trail? What choices would you have made along the way? Do you think you would have survived?

This book is full of questions that relate to the Oregon Trail. Some are questions real people had to face. The questions are followed by details to help you come to a decision.

THE OREGON TRAIL

Oregon

Missouri

Pick one choice or the other. There are no wrong answers! But just like the pioneers, you should think carefully about your decisions.

Are you ready? Turn the page to pick this or that!

THIS

To travel in a
LARGE WAGON TRAIN?

- ➤ as many as 100 wagons
- ➤ harder to organize
- ➤ greater possibility of fighting among a large group

Pioneers traveled in groups called wagon trains. Some wagon trains were large. One had more than 120 wagons! Large wagon trains meant more people and animals to organize. This could slow down travel. People in wagon trains also chose leaders. The larger a wagon train, the more people to fight over leadership and other issues. Sometimes, these fights led to severe injuries.

To travel in a

SMALL WAGON TRAIN?

➤ as few as three wagons

➤ less protection

➤ less likely to have people along with special skills

A small wagon train could move quickly. This was important, as pioneers timed their journey to climb the Rocky Mountains before it snowed. But small trains were less likely to have trained doctors or other experts. Wagon trains often circled up at night. This helped the pioneers feel safe from wild animals and **thieves**. Smaller wagon trains had fewer wagons to provide security.

Would you choose . . .

THIS

To
FLOAT YOUR WAGON
across a river?

➤ pull wagon across the river yourself

➤ takes a long time to unload and reload

➤ supplies could wash away

To float a wagon, pioneers first had to empty its contents. Then they took the wagon box off the wheels and **caulked** it. Finally, everything was loaded back in the box. Pioneers then floated the wagon across the river. Floating was slow and hard work. If the river was too high or moving fast, it could wash supplies or even people away.

To pay for a wagon
FERRY?

➤ expensive

➤ waiting period

➤ could affect your ability to buy supplies later

Ferries could take pioneers across larger rivers. But travelers often had to wait days in line to ride them. Ferries were also expensive. Pioneers usually did not have money to spare. Spending money on a ferry meant less money for food and supplies for the rest of the journey. This could lead to **starvation** or death.

THIS

To get sick with
CHOLERA?

➤ caused by drinking dirty water or eating dirty food

➤ possibility of a quick death

➤ killed more people on the Oregon Trail than any other disease

Cholera was a leading cause of death on the Oregon Trail. Pioneers got cholera from eating food or drinking water that had touched dead animals, animal poop, or human poop. **Bacteria** in the poop caused cholera. Cholera caused people to throw up and get **diarrhea**. It could kill a person in less than 12 hours. However, if cholera victims survived the first 12 to 24 hours, they often recovered.

To get sick with
DIPHTHERIA?

➤ spread through air

➤ makes it hard to breathe

➤ could cause weeks of
suffering before death

Diphtheria was another common trail disease. Pioneers spread it through the air by coughing or sneezing. Bacteria made poison in the sick person's lungs. This made it hard to breathe. Diphtheria could cause **organ** failure and death within weeks. It was possible to recover from diphtheria. But many travelers who got the disease died from it.

To eat "BACON"?

> large pork hunk

> very salty

> must rinse it well to make it edible

Trail bacon wasn't the bacon we know today. It came from large hunks of pork packed in **brine**. The brine helped keep the meat from spoiling. It also made the meat super salty. If pioneers didn't rinse their bacon well, it was too salty to eat!

To eat
HARDTACK?

➤ tough bread

➤ not much flavor

➤ must dip it in water or coffee to make it edible

Hardtack was made from flour, water, and salt. It did not have yeast. This meant it wasn't soft like bread. Hardtack also wasn't flavorful. True to its name, hardtack was hard and tough to chew. Pioneers dipped it in water or coffee to soften it.

To run out of
FOOD SUPPLIES?

➤ become exhausted from no food

➤ hunting could cause accidents

➤ eat gross things to survive

Without food, pioneers could become too sick and exhausted to finish their journey. Hungry pioneers could hunt wild animals. But hunting took time and could result in accidental gunshot wounds. In tough times, some pioneers ate gross things. One family boiled and ate leather. Others cooked dead animals found on the trail.

To run out of spare parts for your
WAGON WHEEL?

> stranded

> reliant on passing wagon trains for parts

> throws off travel schedule

If a wagon wheel broke and there were no parts to fix it, pioneers were stranded. They would have to wait for a passing wagon train that would hopefully give or sell them parts. Being stranded for too long was dangerous. Any delay could put travelers at risk of facing cold and starvation later on.

To take the
SUBLETTE CUTOFF SHORTCUT?

➤ included 40-mile (64 km) stretch of desert

➤ little water or grass

➤ cactus spines hurt feet

Sublette Cutoff was a shortcut passing through the Little Colorado Desert in Wyoming. This desert was a 40-mile (64 km) stretch without much grass or water. Pioneers traveled in the evening to avoid the hot sun. Still, oxen could die of thirst along the way.

To continue on the
MAIN TRAIL?

➤ 46 miles (74 km) longer

➤ takes two-and-a-half days more travel

➤ still have to cross desert

The main trail was 46 miles (74 km) longer than the shortcut. This meant at least two and a half more days of travel. This route was as dry, hot, and dusty as the Little Colorado Desert. While there was more water to drink, the extra miles were tiring.

THIS

To
**TRAVEL IN EARLY
YEARS** *of the trail?*

➤ not as much known about trail

➤ fewer ferries and bridges to cross rivers

➤ not as many trading posts along the route

Pioneers traveling in the trail's early years didn't have guidebooks on where to go or what to bring. There were also not many ferries or bridges to cross rivers. Before 1849, there were no well-established trading posts. Pioneers wanting to trade for extra food or supplies were out of luck.

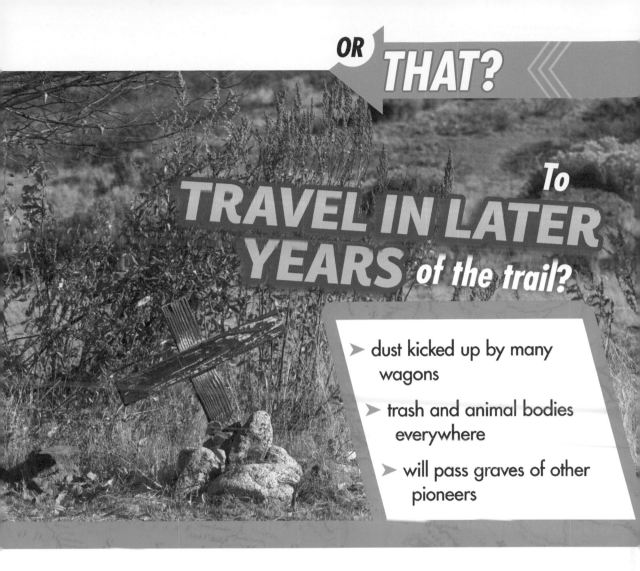

To **TRAVEL IN LATER YEARS** of the trail?

➤ dust kicked up by many wagons

➤ trash and animal bodies everywhere

➤ will pass graves of other pioneers

In later years, the trail was crowded. Wagon trains had to spread out to avoid dust kicked up by other wagon trains. Popular campsites were littered with garbage. Travelers would also pass the bodies of dead oxen and graves of other travelers. People who died on the trail were often buried near it.

THIS

Make a drink at
SODA SPRINGS?

- landmark in Idaho
- bubbly water from volcanic activity
- can sweeten with sugar and drink like soda

For pioneers, reaching a landmark was cause for celebration. Sometimes it was even cause for a special treat! Soda Springs was a landmark in Idaho. Volcanic activity there made the spring water warm and bubbly. Many pioneers added sugar to the water. The resulting drink tasted like soda!

Make a drink at
ICE SPRINGS?

➤ landmark in Wyoming

➤ dig to find ice

➤ can make cold drinks
  or ice cream

Ice Springs was a trail landmark in Wyoming. Marshy plants covered a layer of ice underground that was 10 inches (25 centimeters) thick. This ice stayed frozen through early summer. Pioneers dug up this clear, good-tasting ice. They used it to make cool, refreshing drinks like lemonade. Some even used it to make ice cream!

THIS

To GATHER "BUFFALO CHIPS" *as a chore?*

- ➤ must touch buffalo poop with bare hands
- ➤ must collect a lot
- ➤ smelly

Pioneers built fires to cook. But along some parts of the trail, there was no wood. Pioneers then collected "buffalo chips" for fuel. These "chips" were large, dried pieces of buffalo poop. They burned quickly, so pioneers collected a lot of them—using their bare hands!

To
COOK A MEAL
as a chore?

➤ difficult and slightly dangerous to cook over a fire

➤ could burn your hands

➤ must handle raw meat

Pioneers usually cooked using a Dutch oven. This was a large, heavy pot that grew very hot over a fire. If you weren't careful, you could easily burn your hands. Cooking was also dirty work. It sometimes involved handling raw meat from hunts.

THIS

To be a
DOCTOR?

➤ must see gross injuries

➤ risk of getting sick from patients

➤ few medicines available

Some wagon trains traveled with doctors. These doctors were constantly around gross injuries. Some had to **amputate** people's body parts. Doctors also risked catching diseases from patients. In many cases, there was little a doctor could do to prevent or treat disease. Medical knowledge at the time was basic and many medicines didn't exist yet.

To be a
WAGON DRIVER?

> no seat, so must walk alongside oxen

> no reins to control animals

> could be trampled by oxen

A wagon driver controlled the wagon's oxen by walking alongside the oxen the entire trip and shouting commands. Oxen often got scared by trail sights or sounds. Scared oxen could injure any person nearby. The driver also cared for the oxen. This could be dirty work. Drivers sometimes had to wash dust from inside the oxen's noses and mouths!

To have your foot
BITTEN BY A RATTLESNAKE?

> bites could be deadly if not treated

> painful, swollen wound

> someone might suck out venom from the bite

Rattlesnake bites aren't usually deadly. But the wound swells, making it difficult and painful to walk. A rattlesnake bite could also cause people to throw up and become weak. One way pioneers treated snakebites was to suck and spit out **venom** from the bite. If left untreated, a bite was more likely to cause death.

To have your foot **RUN OVER BY A WAGON WHEEL?**

- swollen, mangled foot
- need a doctor to set broken bones
- can cause a permanent limp

Having your foot crushed by a wagon wheel usually caused broken bones. Then, if you were lucky, a doctor could set the broken foot in a splint. This would help the bones heal. But even with a doctor's help, the bones may heal incorrectly. The injured pioneer may have a limp for the rest of his or her life.

THIS

To travel through DUST?

> irritates eyes

> blows into food

> have to rub axle grease on lips

Dust could be 2 to 3 inches (5 to 8 cm) deep on the trail. It got in people's clothes, eyes, mouths, and food. This dust made the pioneers dirty and was difficult to scrub from clothes. Dry, dusty conditions also caused many pioneers' lips to crack and split. To prevent this, pioneers rubbed axle grease on their lips. This grease was made with tar or animal fat.

OR **THAT?**

To travel through
RAIN?

> wagon wheels get stuck in mud

> slippery to walk

> hard to make campfires

Heavy rains made mud in which wagon wheels could become stuck. Walking in mud was slippery and exhausting for pioneers and animals. Rain also made it uncomfortable to camp. Supplies could get wet. And pioneers couldn't cook dinner if rain put out their fire. In rainy conditions, pioneers often went to bed without a warm meal.

LIGHTNING ROUND

Would you choose to . . .

➤ eat a snake or eat a prairie dog?

➤ deal with an overturned wagon or a runaway wagon?

➤ lose a wagon wheel or lose an ox?

➤ buy new wagon parts or new tools at a fort?

➤ bring a favorite book or favorite toy on the journey?

➤ travel with a cow or travel with chickens?

➤ use downtime to explore the landscape or to keep a diary of the trip?

➤ leave behind cooking pots or wagon repair tools to lighten your wagon?

➤ trade your hunting rifle or blanket for new shoes?

➤ travel on Sundays to make the journey go faster or rest on Sundays to give people and animals a break?

amputate (AM-pyuh-tate)—to cut off someone's limb, usually because it is diseased or damaged

bacterium (bak-TEER-ee-uhm)—a microscopic, single-celled living thing that can either be useful or harmful

brine (BRINE)—seawater, or water that is very salty

caulk (KAWK)—to apply a waterproof material to something in order to prevent it from leaking

diarrhea (dye-uh-REE-uh)—a condition in which normally solid waste from your body becomes liquid

ferry (FER-ee)—a boat that regularly carries people, vehicles, or supplies across a body of water

organ (OR-guhn)—a part of the body, such as the heart or skin, that performs a certain task

pioneer (pye-uh-NEER)—a person who explores unknown territory and settles there

starvation (STAHR-vay-shun)—a state of suffering or cause of death from lack of food

thief (THEEF)—a person who steals others' belongings or money

venom (VEN-uhm)—poison produced by certain animals

READ MORE

Braun, Eric. *Fighting to Survive in the American West: Terrifying True Stories.* North Mankato, MN: Compass Point Books, 2020.

Gregory, Josh. *If You Were a Kid on the Oregon Trail.* New York: Children's Press/Scholastic, 2017.

Wiley, Jesse. *The Race to Chimney Rock.* Boston: Houghton Mifflin Harcourt, 2018.

INTERNET SITES

Ducksters—Westward Expansion: Oregon Trail
https://www.ducksters.com/history/westward_expansion/oregon_trail.php

Scholastic—Explore More with Facts for Now: Pioneer Life
http://www.factsfornow.scholastic.com/article?product_id=nbk&type=0ta&uid=10676833&id=a2023250-h

U.S. Department of the Interior Bureau of Land Management—FAQ's About Kids on the Oregon Trail
https://www.blm.gov/sites/blm.gov/files/learn_interp_nhotic_kidstrail.pdf